Hiroshige

1797-1858

Grange
BOOKS

Text: Michail Uspenski
Translation: Paul Williams

Page 4:
The Suidobashi Bridge and Surugadai (Suidobashi Surugadai),
May 1857.
Colour woodblock print, 36 x 24 cm.
Gift of Anna Ferris, Brooklyn Museum of Art, New York.

Designed by:
Baseline Co Ltd
127-129A Nguyen Hue Bld
Fiditourist, 3rd Floor
District 1, Ho Chi Minh City
Vietnam

© 2007, Sirrocco, London, UK
© 2007, Confidential Concepts, Worldwide, USA

Published in 2007 by Grange Books
an imprint of Grange Books Plc
The Grange Kingsnorth Industrial Estate
Hoo, nr Rochester, Kent ME3 9ND
www.grangebooks.co.uk

ISBN : 978-1-84013-851-1

Printed in China

Foreword

"Dropping my brush at Azuma [Eastern Capital] I go a journey to the honourable country in the west [the Buddhist Paradise is supposed to be in the west] to view the wonderful sights there."

— Hiroshige's death-song which he wrote on a piece of paper.

4

Biography

1797:   Ando Hiroshige was born under the name of Ando Tokutaro. He was the son of the warden of the fire brigade assigned to the Edo Castle. Various episodes indicate that the young Hiroshige was fond of sketching and it is most likely that a fireman, who had studied under a master of the traditional Kano school of painting, oversaw his tutelage.

1809:   His mother died. Shortly after, his father resigned his post, passing it on to his son. Early the following year, his father died as well. Hiroshige's actual daily duties as a fire warden were minimal, and his wages were small.

1811:   At the age of fourteen, the young Hiroshige had the chance to join the famous Utagawa painting school and became a pupil of Utagawa Toyohiro, a famous Japanese *ukiyo-e* artist.

1812:   He obtained a school license and was rewarded with the name Utagawa Hiroshige. In the *ukiyo-e* literature he is usually referenced as Hiroshige Ando.

1818:   His first published work appeared.

1830s:	Hiroshige did not immediately begin to produce landscape prints. His main output consisted of prints of beautiful women (*bijinga*) and actors (*yakushae*). He gradually gave up figure prints for landscapes. He started, under the influence of the great Hokusai, the series that made him famous.
1832:	He traveled between Edo and Kyoto along the famed highway called the Tokaido; he stayed at the 53 overnight stations along the road and made numerous sketches of everything he saw. He published a series of 55 landscape prints entitled the *"Fifty-three Stations on the Tokaido"* - one for each station, as well as the beginning of the highway and the arrival in Kyoto. The success of this series was immediate and made Hiroshige one of the most popular *ukiyo-e* artists of all time.
1850s:	Some vertical-format compilations of landscape prints date from this period such as *"Famous Places in Kyoto"* (1834), *"Eight Views of Lake Biwa"* (1835), *"Sixty-nine Stations on the Kiso Highway"* (c. 1837), and *"One Hundred Famous Views of Edo"* (1856-58).
1858:	Hiroshige died of cholera and was buried in a Zen temple in Asakusa, Tokyo.

Between the seventeenth and nineteenth centuries in Japan, the Edo period (1603-1868), a new tendency in urban art developed and it is to this style, known as *ukiyo-e*, literally *"pictures of the floating world"*, that the woodblock print belongs.

Ando Hiroshige is quite possibly the most famous Japanese print artist beyond his native shores. In 1811 he joined the pupils of one of the prominent print artists of the day, Utagawa Toyohiro. From the turn of the 1830s, Hiroshige's thoughts were more and more concentrated on the landscape, which subsequently became the chief theme of his

Peach, Plum, Chrysanthemum, a Monkey, and Chickens

From the series *Shellwork* from an exhibition at Okuyama in Asakusa
1820
Colour woodblock print, 38 x 25.5 cm
Victoria and Albert Museum, London

9

creative work. Over the course of more than twenty years, the artist produced several series of prints, which demonstrated most vividly his talent in that sphere of art. In the 1850s Hiroshige's work underwent a radical change: the earlier smooth narrative manner gave way to abrupt compositional and chromatic contrasts.

Hiroshige's landscapes represented a new and final stage of development in the *ukiyo-e* landscape print and, more broadly, in the traditional art of Japan. For him, there were no vulgar objects, and in his work any landscape motif reflected in human perception is a means of penetrating the essence of nature, its spirit.

Kanbara, from the series "Fifty-three stages of the Kisokaido"

Tokaido gojusan-tsugi: Kanbara
1835-42
Brocade print, 38 x 25.5 cm
Tokyo National Museum, Tokyo

11

SPRING

The Nihonbashi (the "Bridge of Japan") here functions as a symbol of Edo, then the capital of Japan, and indeed of the country as a whole.

In the year following the construction of the bridge, 1604, Tokugawa Ieyasu issued a decree that assured the importance of the Nihonbashi for posterity: the middle of the bridge became the point from which all distances in the country were to be measured. The area around the Nihonbashi was one of the most important commercial centres in Edo.

A Bright Morning after a Fall of Snow by the Nihonbashi Bridge

Nihonbashi Yukibare
May 1856
Colour woodblock print, 33.7 x 22.5 cm
Gift of Theodore Lande, Art Gallery of Greater Victoria, Vancouver

This view of sailing boats against the dawn background is the one obtained from the tall eminence called Kasumigasekizaka – the Hill of the Outpost of the Mists.

After Edo was made the capital, Tokugawa Ieyasu allocated Kasumigaseki for the residences of powerful members of the feudal hierarchy (*tozama-daimyo*). The prevailing atmosphere on the street is one of merry-making. Hiroshige's depiction of the Outpost of the Mists is indeed set in a festive period, during the New Year celebrations.

The Outpost of the Mists

Kasumigaseki
January 1857
Colour woodblock print, 37 x 23 cm
Gift of Anna Ferris, Brooklyn Museum of Art, New York

15

This print depicts one of the most aristocratic areas of the Eastern Capital – the place known as Hibiya, in the Soto-Sakurada district. Hiroshige places us directly opposite this estate, and the red gates of the house are the first thing to catch our attention. This is considered the most detailed image of a *daimyo* estate in *ukiyo-e* art. Two further details catch the attention: the traditional and most common New Year decoration, *kadomatsu*, a decorated pine in front of the entrance in the foreground, and the kites fluttering in the sky. These are indisputable signs that the start of the New Year is depicted here.

Hibiya in the Soto-Sakurada District, seen from the Yamashita Quarter

Yamashitacho Hibiya Soto-Sakurada
December 1857
Colour woodblock print, 36 x 24 cm
Brooklyn Museum of Art, New York

H ere the viewer is placed in a boat passing beneath the Eitaibashi Bridge. Eitaibashi is the largest bridge and one of the oldest across the Sumidagawa. It was constructed in 1698. The panorama from the bridge developed into one of the traditional themes of Japanese poetry in the Edo period. The bridge was frequently damaged by floods and had to be repaired at considerable expense. Finally, the government decided to give up the struggle and abandon the Eitaibashi.

Tsukudajima Island from the Eitaibashi Bridge

Eitaibashi Tsukudajima
February 1857
Colour woodblock print, 36 x 24 cm
Gift of Anna Ferris, Brooklyn Museum of Art, New York

The white summit of Mount Fuji rises from a scarlet strip of dawn sky. The even line of houses belonging to common people that forms the background of the print is disrupted only by the slight curve of the bridge built across the Yagenbori canal, at the point where it joins the Sumidagawa. This bridge is known as Moto-Yanagibashi – the "True Willow Bridge". At this early hour, boats are passing along the Sumidagawa loaded with goods for the numerous markets that open while it is still dark.

The Ekoin Monastery at Ryogoku and the
Moto-Yanagibashi Bridge

Ryogoku Ekoin Motoyanagibashi
May 1857
Colour woodblock print, 36 x 24 cm
Gift of Anna Ferris, Brooklyn Museum of Art, New York

In the early Edo period this spot, like the whole of the Bakurocho quarter, was the scene of lively horse-dealing. In front of the area of hostelries lay the Hatsune-no baba racetrack, the oldest in Edo. The site was directly connected with the Battle of Sekigahara in 1600 that brought the Tokugawa house to power. With time, the character of the place changed. Together with Bakurocho, it became a centre for working and selling fabrics.

The Hatsune-no baba Racetrack in the Bakurocho Quarter

Bakurocho Hatsune-no baba
September 1857
Colour woodblock print, 36 x 24 cm
Gift of Anna Ferris, Brooklyn Museum of Art, New York

From the second half of the seventeenth century, merchants trading in fabrics began to concentrate their businesses in this quarter. Hiroshige shows us First Street from the gate which closed off the quarter. From the moment the new capital was founded, gates like these were installed in all the quarters of Edo for crime prevention and, most importantly, fire prevention.

The Street of Fabric Shops in the Odemmacho Quarter

Odemmacho momendana
April 1858
Colour woodblock print, 36 x 24 cm
Gift of Anna Ferris, Brooklyn Museum of Art, New York

25

A street straight as an arrow runs right to the very foot of Mount Fuji, which is depicted in the centre of the print. The mountain is separated from the cityscape by a strip of stylised clouds that Hiroshige "borrowed" from the repertoire of classical painting: Fuji seems to exist in a different world. It reigns above the urban bustle of the commercial quarter near the Nihonbashi, without coming into contact with it.

The Surugacho Quarter

Surugacho
September 1856
Colour woodblock print, 36 x 24 cm
Gift of Anna Ferris, Brooklyn Museum of Art, New York

In 1636, the Sujikai-gomon gate was constructed on the road leading from the Nihonbashi bridge to Ueno, for the inspection of travellers. Next to a *daimyo*'s mansion is a small guardhouse, which Hiroshige depicted in the upper left-hand part of the print. Quite possibly this mansion is the destination of a procession consisting of several palanquins (*kago*), servants carrying luggage baskets and samurai guards. On the other side of the Kandagawa we can see the majestic buildings of the Kanda-myojin, one of the most popular Shinto holy places among those born and bred in the city.

Yatsukoji Square seen from the Sujikai Gate

Sujikai-uchi Yatsukoji
November 1857
Colour woodblock print, 34 x 23 cm
Brooklyn Museum of Art, New York

This print takes the viewer onto the grounds of the Kanda-myojin shrine. The shrine was one of the most ancient in Edo. It had been founded in the year 730 in the village of Shibasaki (the present-day Otemachi quarter). The shrine was held to be the dwelling-place of the spirits, who guarded the capital. Perhaps for that reason the Kanda-matsuri temple festival was the most popular holiday among the natives of the city. The print, though, depicts something different – the quiet start to a day of noise and bustle, which all days were in the Eastern Capital's most frequently-visited holy place.

The Kanda-myojin Shrine at Daybreak

Kanda-myojin akebono-no kei
September 1857
Colour woodblock print, 34 x 23 cm
Gift of Anna Ferris, Brooklyn Museum of Art, New York

神田神
社の景

Kiyomizudo was the most important of the temples of the Kanyeiji monastery, one of the main Buddhist centres in the Eastern Capital.

In the print Hiroshige has placed the red terrace wreathed in the cherry blossom of spring in the foreground. From it there is a view of the Shinobazu-no ike. Hiroshige depicted Kiyomizudo in spring, when it is literally swimming in white cherry blossom. The cherry trees, which had already been planted by the third shogun, Iemitsu, were a local prodigy and brought Ueno fame as the best place for the admiration of the spring blossom (*hanami*).

The Kiyomizudo Temple and Shinobazu Pond at Ueno

Ueno Kiyomizudo Shinobazu-no ike
April 1856
Colour woodblock print, 33.7 x 22.5 cm
Gift of Theodore Lande, Art Gallery of Greater Victoria,
Vancouver

Yamashita, literally "below the hill", was an area of wasteland at the foot of Ueno hill. It was supposed to serve as a fire-break and was deliberately created in 1737. In overpopulated Edo empty spaces were at a very high premium. Soon various eating-houses, wine-shops and restaurants appeared here (one of which is depicted on the right-hand side of the engraving). Directly beneath the *suyarigasumi* (white and pink stylised clouds), surrounded by trees lower down the slope stands a fairly small structure heralded by a *torii* gate. This is Gojo-tenjin, a Shinto shrine dedicated to Sugawara-no Mitizane (845-903), a minister and poet, the deified patron of scholars and students.

Yamashita at Ueno

Ueno Yamashita
August 1858
Colour woodblock print, 36 x 23 cm
Gift of Anna Ferris, Brooklyn Museum of Art, New York

U eno hill was one of the main centres of attraction in the Eastern Capital. The word Shitaya ("lower valley") was used to describe a fairly extensive area at the foot of Ueno Hill. A group of women carrying parasols is making its way up the middle of the hill. Most probably they are on a trip to admire the cherry blossoms at Kanyeiji. The women are followed by three samurai who wear European-style trousers. This trend began in the late 1850s and became almost the norm by the next decade, the start of the Meiji period (1868-1912) which saw the rapid penetration of western culture into all spheres of Japanese life.

Hirokoji Street in the Shitaya District

Shitaya hirokoji
September 1856
Colour woodblock print, 36 x 23 cm
Gift of Anna Ferris, Brooklyn Museum of Art, New York

Nippori was part of one of the quietest areas of the Eastern Capital, lying between Ueno and another hill. The name means "the village of life, day in, day out", suggesting a calm, unhurried existence. Until the 1670s and 1680s, there was nothing remarkable about the place, but then several existing monasteries and Shinto shrines moved here and others were constructed. Hiroshige takes us to the Shushoin monastery belonging to the Nichiren school, which was founded in 1575 and moved to Nippori in 1668. The Shushoin monastery was a favourite place of relaxation among the inhabitants of Edo.

Landscaped Gardens at the Nippori Temple

Nippori jiin-no rinsen
February 1857
Colour woodblock print, 36 x 24 cm
Gift of Anna Ferris, Brooklyn Museum of Art, New York

Here we find ourselves in the grounds of the Shinto shrine Suwa-myojin, which was believed to protect two neighbouring places, Yanaka and Nippori. The latter appears in the print: a fairly steep slope leads to a group of buildings half-hidden by masses of cherry blossom. The Suwa-myojin shrine was founded in 1205. Later visitors were, to a large extent, attracted by the views to be had from the Suwanodai promontory. It is one of these views that Hiroshige presents.

Suwa Bluff at Nippori

Nippori Suwanodai
May 1856
Colour woodblock print, 36 x 24 cm
Gift of Anna Ferris, Brooklyn Museum of Art, New York

It is believed that the name Sendagi – "1000 Bundles of Firewood" – came from the trade practised by the local peasants: they cut firewood in the surrounding woods and then brought it to Edo, 1000 bundles at a time. This formerly rural area was only incorporated into the city in 1745.

In the upper part of the print a steep flight of steps, flanked by stone lamps and artificial rocks, leads to a tall pavilion. Space in this print is divided by stylised clouds like those frequently found in ancient Japanese painting.

The Pavilion of Flowers on Dangozaka Slope, the Sendagi Quarter

Sendagi Dangozaka Hanayashiki
May 1856
Colour woodblock print, 36 x 24 cm
Gift of Anna Ferris, Brooklyn Museum of Art, New York

Admiring the cherry blossoms was one of the most traditional and popular pastimes for the Japanese in the nineteenth century and remains so today. Four places were most frequented for *hanami*: Ueno, Gotenyama, the bank of the Sumidagawa and Asukayama, the hill depicted in this print. The name of the hill came from a small Shinto shrine that was founded as early as 1321-1324. Despite being over three miles from the centre of the city, it became one of the most popular places to spend time in the bosom of nature, particularly in the cherry blossom season.

The View North from Asukayama Hill

Asukayama kita-no chobo
May 1856
Colour woodblock print, 36 x 24 cm
Gift of Anna Ferris, Brooklyn Museum of Art, New York

O ji Inari-jinja was a well-preserved ancient shrine, dating back to before the Edo period. Inari, originally a harvest deity, was later redefined as the bringer of prosperity and success in one's affairs, including commerce. Once a year, during the temple festival on the 1st Day of the Horse in the Second Month, the shrine was associated with something else. The day was known as the kite fair (*tako-no ichi*). This festival also had an agricultural origin, as a ritual to protect the coming harvest.

The Inari Shrine at Oji

Oji Inari-no yashiro
September 1857
Colour woodblock print, 36 x 24 cm
Brooklyn Museum of Art, New York

In 1657, this dam was built north of Asukayama for irrigation purposes. During the Edo period, the monastery enjoyed the particular attention of the Tokugawa family, but in the Meiji period it was abandoned and today only two of its buildings still exist. The water spilling over the dam was commonly referred to as Otaki, "the great waterfall". In actual fact, it was considerably more modest in size than is shown here. Possibly not only compositional considerations, but also the popular name prompted Hiroshige to exaggeration.

The Dam on the Otonashi River at Oji, popularly known as "The Great Waterfall"

Oji Otonashigawa entai sezoku Otaki to tonau
February 1857
Colour woodblock print, 36 x 24 cm
Brooklyn Museum of Art, New York

This ferry across the Sumidagawa was in the northern outskirts of Edo. It served pilgrims seeking to visit the Zenkoji monastery.

Once, a monk named Teison was visited in his sleep by the Amida Buddha venerated in Zenkoji (Shinano province), who instructed the monk to make an exact image of him. Teison moulded a sculptural group of three figures: the Amida Buddha and two accompanying bodhisattvas, Kannon and Seishi. This work was completed in 1195 and the composition was placed in a temple, which became known as Zenkoji.

The Zenkoji Monastery by the Kawaguchi Ferry

Kawaguchi-no watashi Zenkoji
February 1857
Colour woodblock print, 36 x 24 cm
Gift of Anna Ferris, Brooklyn Museum of Art, New York

51

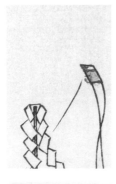

M ount Atago stands to the east of Yamanote, an aristocratic section of the city containing the mansions of *daimyo* and high-ranking samurai. It got its name from the Atago-jinja or Atago-gongen shrine constructed on its summit. The most famous and popular festival at Atago-jinja was called Bishamon-matsuri and dedicated to Bishamon-ten, the guardian of the North in the Buddhist pantheon and one of the seven gods of happiness in popular belief.

Mount Atago, the Shiba District

Shiba Atagoyama
August 1857
Colour woodblock print, 36 x 24 cm
Brooklyn Museum of Art, New York

53

Until the mid-nineteenth century Hiroo was a rural locality in the Shibuya district to the north-west of Edo. Only towards the very end of the Edo period did people begin to build teahouses and restaurants there. It became a destination for day-trippers out to see "untouched nature".

In the 1850s the main attraction of Hiroo was the restaurant, originally called Owariya, which stood where Hiroshige depicted it, on the left bank of the Furukawa. The speciality of the house was an eel dish, highly prized in the Eastern Capital.

The Furukawa River at Hiroo

Hiroo Furukawa
July 1856
Colour woodblock print, 34 x 24 cm
Gift of Anna Ferris, Brooklyn Museum of Art, New York

In Hiroshige's time, Meguro was part of the quiet outskirts of forests and fields. From time to time the shoguns practised falconry here, while in spring the peasants gathered young bamboo shoots which they sold by the gate of the Ryusenji monastery.

The history of the monastery goes back to the time of Ieyasu and his great adviser Tenkai, the monk who founded Kanyeiji. Tenkai believed that the new capital should be protected by divine forces as well as men, and he gave instructions for the building of five outlying monasteries. Meguro Fudo was the largest of the monasteries and considered the most important.

The Chiyogaike Pond at Meguro

Meguro Chiyogaike
July 1856
Colour woodblock print, 36 x 24 cm
Gift of Anna Ferris, Brooklyn Museum of Art, New York

There were two structures connected with one of the most popular cults in Japanese folk religion, that of Mount Fuji. One of them, Shin-Fuji ("New Fuji"), is shown here. The cult of Fuji has its roots in mythological time. Pilgrimages up the mountain began in the ninth century and by the Edo period had become more common.

The New Fuji at Meguro that Hiroshige depicted in the present print was raised in 1829. It took the form of an earth mound overgrown with grass.

New Fuji at Meguro

Meguro Shin-Fuji
April 1857
Colour woodblock print, 36 x 24 cm
Brooklyn Museum of Art, New York

59

T wo *fuji-zuka* were put up at Meguro in the early part of the nineteenth century. The New Fuji was new in relation to the other artificial mountain constructed 17 years earlier, in 1812, less than a mile to the north. After the appearance of a second *fuji-zuka*, the older mound became known as Moto-Fuji, "the Original Fuji". Moto-Fuji was intended not so much as a setting for the practice of religious ritual but as a pleasant place to spend time admiring the views across the water-meadows of the Megurogawa river.

The Original Fuji at Meguro

Meguro Moto-Fuji
April 1857
Colour woodblock print, 36 x 24 cm
Gift of Anna Ferris, Brooklyn Museum of Art, New York

This print is a rare example of how, over the course of the series, Hiroshige "left the capital", depicting its more distant outskirts.

In Hiroshige's time, Hakkeizaka was adorned by a gigantic pine of eccentric shape.

The very name "Hanging-Armour Pine" evoked associations with Japan's martial past. There was a legend that, during his campaign against the insurgent Abe-no Sadato (1019-1062), Hatimantaro Yoshiie (1041-1108), the outstanding military commander of the late Heian period, stopped to rest here and hung his armour on one of the pines.

The "Hanging-Armour Pine" and Hakkeizaka

Hakkeizaka Yoroikakematsu
May 1856
Colour woodblock print, 36 x 24 cm
Brooklyn Museum of Art, New York

The Kamata district was particularly noted for its abundant plum trees, which created an attractive spectacle when they blossomed in early spring. Horticultural, Kamata reached the peak of its fame in the Bunsei era (1818-1830) when a special garden was laid out in the grounds of Namekata Danjo's house, which became known as Umeyashiki, the "Plum Mansion". Despite being private property, the garden was open to the public: teahouses, taverns and leisure establishments appeared here.

The Plum Orchard in Kamata

Kamata-no umezono
February 1857
Colour woodblock print, 36 x 24 cm
Gift of Anna Ferris, Brooklyn Museum of Art, New York

名所江戸百景

蒲田の梅園

65

The Shinagawa district was the starting point for those heading for Kyoto, Nara and Osaka on the Tokaido highway. Shinagawa was marked by two eminences – Yatsuyama and Gotenyama. The latter translates as "palace hill" and for several centuries there really was a palace on the hill.

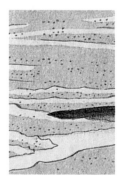

The Gotenyama in Shinagawa

Shinagawa Gotenyama
April 1856
Colour woodblock print, 36 x 24 cm
Gift of Anna Ferris, Brooklyn Museum of Art, New York

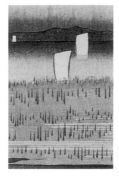

In the Edo period the name Sunamura referred to an area adjoining Edo Bay. The area lay beneath the sea until in 1659 Sunamura Shinjiro carried out work to drain part of the bay. The reclaimed land was named after him.

Hiroshige avoided directly presenting the place which, according to the title, was the main subject of the print. By the early nineteenth century Moto-Hachiman had become a place for the inhabitants of Edo to stroll.

Moto-Hachiman Shrine, Sunamura

Sunamura Moto-Hachiman
April 1856
Colour woodblock print, 36 x 24 cm
Gift of Anna Ferris, Brooklyn Museum of Art, New York

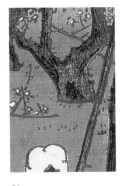

In the Edo period Kameido still lay outside the city. The easiest way to reach it was by water, along the Jikkengawa canal, past Yanagishima with its noted temple, to the bodhisattva Myoken and Hashimotoya teahouse. One unusual plum tree was particularly famous – the Garyubai ("Reclining Dragon"). This print was destined to play a role in the history of Western painting. Vincent van Gogh copied it, studying the visual devices, compositional structure and emotional charge of *ukiyo-e* prints, which at that time were perceived as the most characteristically Japanese art form.

The Plum Orchard in Kameido

Kameido Umeyashiki
November 1857
Colour woodblock print, 34 x 23 cm
Gift of Anna Ferris, Brooklyn Museum of Art, New York

The real subject of this print is the Jikkengawa canal, with cherry trees evenly spaced along its bank. Jikkengawa means "the Ten-Ken River" (1 *ken* = 6 feet). In reality it was a canal, dug in the Manji era (1856-1860) to link the Sumidagawa and Nakagawa, the two most important rivers in the Eastern Capital.

The composition is arranged so that the viewer's eye is drawn along the bank, past rice paddies, to the Shinto shrine in the depths of the picture.

The Conjoined Camphor Trees by the Azuma-no mori Shrine

Azuma-no mori Renri-no azusa
July 1856
Colour woodblock print, 36 x 24 cm
Gift of Anna Ferris, Brooklyn Museum of Art, New York

Hiroshige shows us a built-up area at the junction of two canals. The Kita-Jikkengawa, running from top to bottom, is crossed at right-angles by the Yoko-Jikkengawa. These waterways played a substantial role in the transport system of the Northern Capital, linking a network of rivers and canals to the Sumidagawa, the city's main artery. Soon the area around the bridge became one of the liveliest amusement centres for the capital's populace. It was from here that boats departed for the "pleasure quarters" of Fukagawa and Shin-Yoshiwara, as well as to Mukojima.

Yanagishima

─────────────

Yanagishima
April 1857
Colour woodblock print, 36 x 24 cm
Robert O. Muller Collection, New York

This print takes us into the distant north-western approaches to Edo. The canal depicted was created in the early seventeenth century to supply the Fukagawa district with drinking water. A hundred years later it was used only for irrigation and as a means of conveying freight, mainly agricultural produce. In time, pleasure boats also appeared – little barges carrying two or three passengers and drawn by a man walking on the bank.

Tow Boats on the Yotsugidori Canal

Yotsugidori yosui hikifune
February 1857
Colour woodblock print, 36 x 23 cm
Gift of Anna Ferris, Brooklyn Museum of Art, New York

For Hiroshige's contemporaries, Matsuyama was firmly connected with a visit to Yoshiwara, the most famous and expensive "green quarter" in Japan, which was noted for its beautiful courtesans. In Hiroshige's print, we look at Matsuchiyama temple from the other bank of the Sumidagawa, which is called simply Mukojima, the "Island Opposite" – opposite Asakusa. Close to the spot depicted was the Mimeguri-jinja, a Shinto shrine noted for its cherry trees.

Night View of Matsuchiyama and the Sanyabori Canal

Matsuchiyama Sanyabori yakei
August 1857
Colour woodblock print, 36 x 24 cm
Gift of Anna Ferris, Brooklyn Museum of Art, New York

Suijin-no mori is dedicated to the Sumidagawa. Here they venerated the dragon who ruled the watery element, the defender and master of the river. The choice of site was no coincidence – at one time the mouth of the Sumidagawa was situated here.

The place shown on the opposite bank is Massaki, which was noted for its shrines, the first and foremost of which was Massaki Inari-jinja, dedicated to the god of the harvest, and its teahouses.

The dominant element in the composition is Tsukubayama, depicted in the distance, almost in the centre of the page.

Massaki and the Suijin-no mori Shrine on the Sumidagawa

Sumidagawa Suijin-no mori Massaki
August 1856
Colour woodblock print, 36 x 24 cm
Gift of Anna Ferris, Brooklyn Museum of Art, New York

The "green quarters" of Yoshiwara were one of the most important sights of the Eastern Capital. A stop at Massaki was a virtual "must". Through the round window, the *shoji* shutters of which have not been completely opened, we have a view of the Sumidagawa and the opposite bank. The twin peaks of this mountain were known as "male" (western) and "female" (eastern). In myths, ancient tales and folk beliefs, it functioned as a symbol of unbreakable fidelity and all-conquering love.

View from the Massaki Shrine of the Uchigawa Sekiya-no sato Village and the Suijin-no mori Shrine

Massaki-hen yori Suijin-no mori Utagawa Sekiya-no sato
August 1857
Colour woodblock print, 36 x 24 cm
Gift of Anna Ferris, Brooklyn Museum of Art, New York

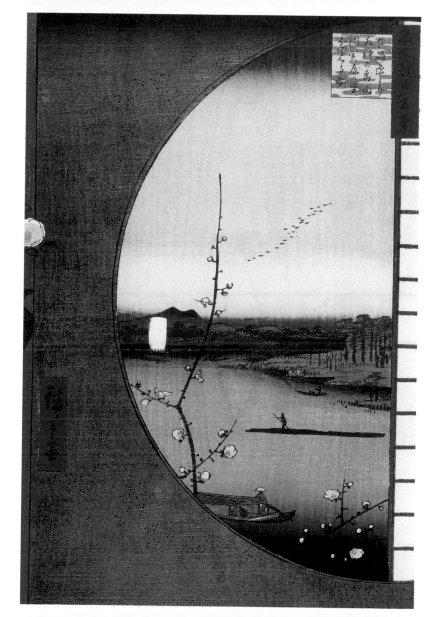

H ere Hiroshige places us in Asakusa on the west bank of the Sumidagawa. The print accurately shows two boats making the crossing, one in each direction. We find ourselves alongside the kilns that were used to bake tiles and simple pieces of pottery. These products were called *imado-yaki*, from the Imado area, which extended quite a way along the Sumidagawa.

Besides associations with everyday life, the view Hiroshige depicts could have had contemporaries recollecting classical literature. The key element here is the birds floating on the river. They are *miyakodori*, "birds of the capital".

Tile Kilns by the Hashiba-no watashi Ferry on the Sumidagawa River

Sumidagawa Hashiba-no watashi kawaragama
April 1857
Colour woodblock print, 36 x 24 cm
Gift of Anna Ferris, Brooklyn Museum of Art, New York

E do was created as a city for soldiers in service, either with the shogun or one of the *daimyo* whose duties included being present in the capital for a fixed period.

At the start of the Edo period, the Eastern Capital was a "masculine city", its population made up of warriors and burghers – merchants, craftsmen and those who served them. This all created a favourable climate for ladies of easy virtue, and that aspect of life could have spiralled out control, threatening the state policy of strict control in all spheres.

Dawn in the "Green Quarters"

Kakuchu shinonome
April 1857
Colour woodblock print, 36 x 24 cm
Brooklyn Museum of Art, New York

The main feature of this print is Kinryuzan, literally "the mountain of the golden dragon" – the "mountain name" (*zango*) of the Sensoji Monastery. Here the red five-tier pagoda and massive *hondo* can be seen in the middle distance on the right. The foreground of the print is occupied by part of a *yanebune* (or *yakatabune*), a covered pleasure boat. Passengers were entertained by geishas who served them wine and food and performed songs to the accompaniment of the *shamisen*, the three-stringed lute. The presence of people in the scene is barely indicated: the figure of one of the geishas (there should have been at least two) is abruptly cut off by the left-hand edge.

Distant View of the Kinryuzan and the Azumabashi Bridge

Azumabashi Kinryuzan enbo
August 1857
Colour woodblock print, 36 x 24 cm
Gift of Anna Ferris, Brooklyn Museum of Art, New York

The Kanda aqueduct was one of the largest canals supplying the capital with water for drinking and other purposes. The area was included in the city as the Sekiguchi-daimachi district in 1720. The great adornment of this suburb was Camellia Hill (Tsubakiyama). Another attraction of the district was the Suijinsha shrine on the top of the hill, which was dedicated to the water deity Mizuka-no me.

In the print, Hiroshige manages to convey the spirit of poetry and the atmosphere of thoughtful contemplation.

The Bashoan Retreat on Tsubakiyama near the Aqueduct in the Sekiguchi Quarter

Sekiguchi jôsuibata Bashôan Tsubakiyama
April 1857
Colour woodblock print, 36 x 24 cm
Brooklyn Museum of Art, New York

In this print we find ourselves back near the shogun's castle on the bank of the Sotobori, the "External Moat" that cut right across the city. The area around the castle was for the most part occupied by the mansions of major feudal lords. The composition is dominated by an ensemble – the Hachiman-jinja, one of the oldest Shinto shrines in Edo. It was founded in the fifteenth century, but soon destroyed by war and restored by Tokugawa Ieyasu. The shrine, dedicated to Hachiman, the Shinto god of war and the most powerful protector of Buddhism, was noted in Hiroshige's day for its bells.

The Hachiman Shrine in Ichigaya

Ichigaya Hachiman
October 1858
Colour woodblock print, 33.7 x 22.2 cm
Achenbach Foundation for Graphic Arts, Fine Arts Museums
of San Francisco, San Francisco

市ヶ谷
八幡

広重画

This print takes us to a district called Shinjuku located by the Tamagawa, a twenty-mile-long canal that supplied a considerable part of Edo with drinking water. In Hiroshige's day, the banks of the canal were occupied by the properties of *daimyo*. On the left is the entrance to the mansion of the Naito clan, who played a major part in the formation of the district. The district flourished for some twenty years, until a special government decree forbade all commercial activity in Shinjuku.

Cherry Trees in Blossom on the Tamagawa
Embankment

Tamagawa zutsumi-no hana
February 1856
Colour woodblock print, 36.4 x 24.7 cm
Private collection

SUMMER

The area around the Nihonbashi Bridge held a special attraction for all the inhabitants of Edo. It was the focal point of the daily activities of merchants and craftsmen, who gave rise to one of the most original phenomena in Japanese cultural life – *chonin-no bunka*, the culture of townspeople. Between the Nihonbashi and Edobashi, there were markets on both sides of the river. The white-plastered warehouses in the upper part of the print were if not a sight, then a feature of the locality. Aomono-ichiba, the Green (vegetable) Market that began near the Nihonbashi, was the destination for most of the freight laden boats seen in the print.

The Nihonbashi and Edobashi Bridges

Nihonbashi Edobashi
December 1857
Colour woodblock print, 33.8 x 22.1 cm
Achenbach Foundation for Graphic Arts, Fine Arts Museums
of San Francisco, San Francisco

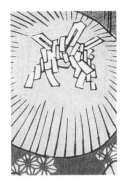

The Nihonbashi district was a flourishing centre of trade and crafts. The samurai, the ruling military class, did not live here. It was the preserve of the merchant class, at least of its more successful, and at times fabulously wealthy, members. Suffice it to mention such businesses as Mitsubishi, Mitsui and Mitsukoshi, which are still household names today. Nihonbashi was also noted as the focal point of Edo's distinctive urban culture, which gave the literary world Saikaku and Bakin, and the fine arts a whole galaxy of *ukiyo-e* artists.

First Street in the Nihonbashi District

Nihonbashi tori Itchôme ryakuzu
August 1858
Colour woodblock print, 36 x 24 cm
Gift of Anna Ferris, Brooklyn Museum of Art, New York

Yatsumi-no hashi can be translated as "the Bridge of Eight Views": it affords attractive views in all directions. It was surrounded by a variety of enterprises, workshops and shops. Across the Nihonbashigawa, we see another bridge – the Zenikamebashi. From the early days of Edo as the capital, this bridge was noted for the various monetary operations on offer nearby. The area around the Zenikamebashi remains the financial centre of Tokyo today.

Yatsumi Bridge

Yatsumi-no hashi
August 1856
Colour woodblock print, 36 x 24 cm
Gift of Anna Ferris, Brooklyn Museum of Art, New York

The area around the ferry was in no way remarkable, and can hardly have excited the interest of Hiroshige's contemporaries. The bustle of daily life was to be found here too, on this stretch of the Nihonbashi and in the twin quarters of Koamicho and Kayabacho that lined its banks. Both were inhabited by merchants and were active centres of trade. The speciality of Koamicho was wholesale trade.

The Yoroi-no watashi Ferry to the Koamicho Quarter

Yoroi-no watashi Koamichô
October 1857
Colour woodblock print, 34 x 23 cm
Brooklyn Museum of Art, New York

This was the most "Chinese" place in the Japanese capital. The bridge, the steep slope called Shoheizaka and the boundary wall of Seido were all connected with Confucius, the originator of the world's oldest state ideology, the father of the "Chinese tradition". The bridge was built across it in the 1640s. Confucianism was known in Japan at least from the seventh century, and in the Edo period it was adopted as the established state ideology and an official branch of learning.

The Shoheibashi Bridge, the Temple of Confucius and the Kandagawa

Shôheibashi Seidô Kandagawa
September 1857
Colour woodblock print, 36 x 24 cm
Allen Memorial Art Museum, Oberlin College, National
Gallery of Australia, Canberra

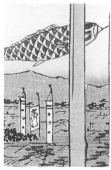

Mount Fuji, the sacred symbol of Japan, could be seen from almost everywhere in old Edo, but the finest view was from Surugadai hill in the Kanda district. The panoramic view of the mansions of "the shogun's immediate vassals" unfolds at the foot of Mount Fuji. The carp depicted in this way were called *shusse-no uo*, "the fish of success", an ancient and lofty symbol. In both China and Japan, the carp was considered the only fish capable of climbing a waterfall on its way upstream, after which, according to legend, it turned into a dragon.

The Suidobashi Bridge and Surugadai

Suidobashi Surugadai
May 1857
Colour woodblock print, 36 x 24 cm
Gift of Anna Ferris, Brooklyn Museum of Art, New York

107

O ji became widely associated, in the first decades of the nineteenth century with the flourishing of its Shinto shrine to the harvest god, Oji Inari-jinja. Pilgrims were attracted by the large number of natural cascades in the area of the shrines on Mount Asuka, the celebrated "Seven Waterfalls of Oji". The most popular of them was named in honour of Fudo, a protective deity that cleared evil spirits and all sorts of obstacles from the path of believers with fire and the sword. In Hiroshige's work this waterfall acquired enormous proportions.

The Fudo Waterfall, Oji

Oji Fudo-no taki
September 1857
Colour woodblock print, 36 x 24 cm
Gift of Anna Ferris, Brooklyn Museum of Art, New York

I n the Edo period the village of Tsunohazu lay on the western outskirts of Edo, on the Koshukaido, one of the country's five great highways. In the nineteenth century it would have been wholly undistinguished had it not been for the Kumano Junisha shrine, one of the oldest in Edo, which Hiroshige depicts in the bottom part of the print.

The Kumano Junisha Shrine at Tsunohazu, popularly known as Juniso

Tsunohazu Kumano Junishâ zokushô Juniso
July 1856
Colour woodblock print, 36 x 24 cm
Gift of Anna Ferris, Brooklyn Museum of Art, New York

111

S anno-matsuri was the main festival of the Hie-jinja Shinto shrine, located in the very centre of Tokyo. The shrine had a long history going back to ninth-century Kyoto. In the Edo period it became the family shrine of the Tokugawa line. The festival took place every year, and was an enormously expensive display. Once laws against excessive luxury were introduced and the procession became more modest, but Sanno-matsuri remained (and still remains) one of the city's favourite festivals.

Sanno Festival Procession on First Street in the Kojimachi Quarter

Kojimachi-itchôme Sanno-matsuri nerikomi
July 1856
Colour woodblock print, 36 x 24 cm
Gift of Anna Ferris, Brooklyn Museum of Art, New York

H iroshige places us on the south bank of the Tameike pond in centrally-located Akasaka, between the large trees that gave the locality its name – Kiribatake, "the Plantation (Field) of Paulownias". These attractive trees of the figwort family were planted around the man-made pond in the early eighteenth century, but some hundred years later, in 1811, most of them were felled. Dwelling houses and leisure establishments appeared here.

The Plantation of Paulownias in Akasaka

Akasaka Kiribatake
April 1856
Colour woodblock print, 36 x 24 cm
Gift of Anna Ferris, Brooklyn Museum of Art, New York

The Zojoji monastery was the most important and influential centre of the Jodoshu (Pure Earth) school in Edo. It occupied an enormous area. Its annual income was roughly as much as that of some provinces and there were more than 3,000 novice monks were studying there at any one time. It owed its success to very close ties with the ruling dynasty, which began with its foundation by Tokugawa Ieyasu.

Pagoda of the Zojoji Monastery and Akabane

Zojojito Akabane
January 1857
Colour woodblock print, 36 x 24 cm
Gift of Anna Ferris, Brooklyn Museum of Art, New York

H ere again we are in the very centre of the city, close to the shogun's castle. Sakurada literally means "Cherry Field" and one of the works of the Tokugawa era states: "Rice paddies extend from the Toranomon gate to the outskirts of Atago. On the boundaries between the fields there are cherry trees, numbering several hundred thousand." Kojimachi is one of the most ancient places in the city.

The Benkeibori Canal from Soto-Sakurada Looking Towards Kojimachi

Soto-Sakurada Benkeibori Kojimachi
May 1856
Colour woodblock print, 33.5 x 21.8 cm
Gift of Anna Ferris, Brooklyn Museum of Art, New York

Tsukudajima was one of two islands in the mouth of the Sumidagawa. It got its name in the early seventeenth century when Tokugawa Ieyasu issued a special decree moving thirty-three specialist *shirauo* fishermen here from the village of Tsukudamura. The fishermen brought with them the cult of the deity of the Sumiyoshi shrine, the protector of seafarers. The shrine's real fame was, however, founded on its temple festival – Sumiyoshi-matsuri. Once every three years the immense head of a fantastic lion (*shishi*) and several palanquins (*mikoshi*) were solemnly paraded.

The Sumiyoshi Shrine Festival on Tsukudajima

Tsukudajima Sumiyoshi-no matsuri
July 1857
Colour woodblock print, 34.4 x 22.5 cm
Carlotta Mabury Collection, Fine Arts Museums of San Francisco, San Francisco

F ukagawa lay on the far bank of the Sumidagawa. The quarter did not come under the Edo municipal authorities until the late 1710s, and, therefore, was not so affected by the many strict regulations and bans operating in the capital. It became the home of beautiful courtesans whose only rivals were in Yoshiwara, the sole "green quarter" officially tolerated in Edo. The figure of the turtle placed in the foreground makes a sharp contrast with the idyllic riverscape.

The Mannenbashi Bridge in Fukagawa

Fukagawa Mannenbashi
November 1857
Colour woodblock print, 36 x 24 cm
Gift of Anna Ferris, Brooklyn Museum of Art, New York

Moving down the Sumidagawa, the main river of the Eastern Capital, Hiroshige is gradually bringing us to its mouth. Here, close to the Mannenbashi bridge, a channel called the Hakozakigawa runs off the main river (known here as the Okawa) towards Mount Fuji. The colouring of the mountain is unusual: a black summit and white slopes. Within five years it became perhaps the most popular entertainment district in Edo. In 1789 a government decree aimed at the "correction of morals" ordered Nakazu razed, and it returned to being a sandbar in the bend of the river.

Channels at Mitsumata Wakarenofuchi

Mitsumata Wakarenofuchi
February 1857
Colour woodblock print, 36 x 24 cm
Brooklyn Museum of Art, New York

125

The bridge shown here was built in 1693 by Shogun Tokugawa Tsunayoshi (1646-1709) to link the Nihonbashi district, the established centre of the city, with Fukagawa. It was remarkable for its size, but since the Ryogokubashi, the next bridge up the Sumidagawa, was then called Ohashi (the "Great Bridge"), this one acquired the name Shin-Ohashi – the "New Great Bridge". Hiroshige depicted the Shin-Ohashi in a typical heavy summer shower. Such downpours were called *yudachi* – "evening appearances", as it was believed that Raijin, the thunder god, brought them with him when he appeared on the Earth.

A Sudden Shower on the Ohashi Bridge and Atake

Ohashi Atake-no yudachi
September 1857
Colour woodblock print, 36 x 24 cm
Gift of Anna Ferris, Brooklyn Museum of Art, New York

The Ryogokubashi was one of the main bridges of the Eastern Capital. It was constructed immediately after the devastating fire of 1657, to link the already overpopulated part of the city with the eastern bank of the Sumidagawa. The bridge became a lively centre of amusements. The numerous teahouses and restaurants by the bridge were never quiet, day or night. In the print Hiroshige depicts an everyday scene with the usual bustle: freighters and passenger boats plying the river.

The Ryogokubashi Bridge and Okawabata Bank

Ryogokubashi Okawabata
August 1856
Colour woodblock print, 36 x 24 cm
Gift of Anna Ferris, Brooklyn Museum of Art, New York

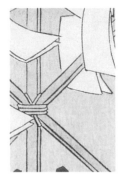

The title here includes three names all used for the lower reaches of the River Arakawa: Asakusagawa, Okawa and Miyatogawa. Hiroshige has depicted one of the seasonal festivals – Oyama-mode, the pilgrimage to Mount Oyama. The initial ceremony of ritual purification took place at the eastern end of the Ryogokubashi. The participants chanted a prayer to the god of the Afuri-jinja shrine, then each of them threw a dry rice stem into the river. If it was carried away by the current, that meant that the prayer had been heard; if it circled on the spot then it was a bad sign.

The Asakusagawa River, Okawabata Bank and Miyatogawa River

Asakusagawa Okawabata Miyatogawa
July 1857
Colour woodblock print, 36 x 24 cm
Gift of Anna Ferris, Brooklyn Museum of Art, New York

Famous pine trees stood in many parts of the Eastern Capital. The Shubi-no Matsu ("Successful Conclusion") was noted for having a shape like a dragon. Its branches spread far out and hung over the Sumidagawa. The original tree was broken by a hurricane in the Anyei era (1772-1780) and replaced by another, a process that was repeated several times. Of all the named pines, Shubi-no matsu is the one most often depicted in engravings, and it is also mentioned in poetry.

The "Shubi-no matsu Pine" and the Ommayagashi Bank on the Asakusagawa River

Asakusagawa Shubi-no matsu Ommayagashi
August 1856
Colour woodblock print, 36 x 24 cm
Gift of Anna Ferris, Brooklyn Museum of Art, New York

Here we are in the precincts of the Komakatado Buddhist temple. The whole temple was dedicated to Kannon and its main sacred image was a sculptural depiction of the bodhisattva in the form of Bato-Kannon (Hayagriva). In the distance we see the Honjo district and the Azumabashi, dating from 1774, one of the four major bridges over the Sumidagawa. A bird hangs in the stormy sky above Komakatado. Its appearance in this print is as a traditional image of the season.

The Komakatado Temple and the Azumabashi Bridge

Komakatado Azumabashi
January 1857
Colour woodblock print, 36 x 24 cm
Gift of Anna Ferris, Brooklyn Museum of Art, New York

There is a story attached to this stretch of water that explains its rather strange name – Kanegafuchi, the "Bell Deep". In the mid-eighteenth century a bell cast in 1735 was being transported by boat from the Choshoji monastery to Hashiba on the opposite bank. In the middle of the river the boat turned over and the bell sank. All attempts to raise it proved futile and the spot became known as the "Bell Deep". This part of the Sumidagawa was considered to have particularly attractive mulberry trees and Hiroshige uses one of them, with pink flowers, as a "side-flap" for the scene he presents.

The Ayasegawa River and Kanegafuchi

Ayasegawa Kanegafuchi
July 1857
Colour woodblock print, 36 x 24 cm
Brooklyn Museum of Art, New York

This print is among the "decorative" works of the series – the exquisite lines of the flowers create a sort of ornamental effect. The vogue for *hanashobu* had reached its height when Hiroshige made this print. About that time the flower became widely known in Europe, where large plantations were established.

The flower also had a certain influence on the fine arts, notably becoming one of the characteristic motifs of *art nouveau*, a movement that absorbed many elements of Japanese artistic tradition.

Irises at Horikiri

Horikiri-no hanashôbu
May 1857
Colour woodblock print, 36 x 24 cm
Gift of Anna Ferris, Brooklyn Museum of Art, New York

139

The foreground in this print consists exclusively of flowering wistaria (*fuji*), a symbol of summer. The Shinto shrine at Kameido was famous for its display of these blooms.

The shrine was dedicated to Sugawara Michizane (845-903), a minister and poet of the Heian period, who was deified after his death, both as patron of scholars and students, and as a thunder-god. The shrine was noted for its garden, a pond in the shape of the character *kokoro* ("heart", "soul") and two bridges indicating the way to Shinden. Such high-arched bridges are known as *taikobashi* – "drum bridges".

In the Precincts of the Tenjin Shrine at Kameido

Kameido Tenjin keidai
July 1856
Colour woodblock print, 36 x 24 cm
Gift of Anna Ferris, Brooklyn Museum of Art, New York

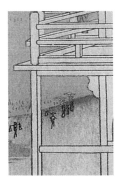

The monastery was situated in the east of Honjo, a new district of the capital. Everything that did not conform, that was strange, unusual or exotic gravitated to the outskirts of the city. The immutable laws of everyday life did not apply here and, in Gohyakurakanji as in Yoshiwara, the result was a topsy-turvy world where the abnormal was the norm. The monastery was founded in the second half of the seventeenth century, but its real rise began in 1696, when Shogun Tsunayoshi granted it land in Honjo.

The "Spiral Temple" in the Monastery of the Five Hundred Rohan

Gohyakurakanji Sazaido
August 1857
Colour woodblock print, 36 x 24 cm
Gift of Anna Ferris, Brooklyn Museum of Art, New York

（題名）
名所江戸百景

芝
羅漢
さゞゐ堂

廣重画

F or the nineteenth-century citizens of Edo, "sights" included architectural monuments, historical relics, popular festivals and ceremonies. A particular place might have been famous for its ephemeral beauties: the full moon, cherry blossoms, summer flowers, and so on. The place shown here is close to the spot where the Tatekawa canal joins the Nakagawa. Travellers headed for, say Narita, had to use the ferry, which took its name from the village visible on the opposite bank.

Sakasai-no watashi Ferry

Sakasai-no watashi
February 1857
Colour woodblock print, 33.9 x 22.7 cm
Gift of Patricia Brown McNamara, Jane Brown Dunaway,
and Helen Brown Jarman
Fine Arts Museums of San Francisco, San Francisco

We are actually in the precincts of the Buddhist monastery Eitaiji, which was famed for its garden. Each year, an "Opening of the Mountain" ceremony (*yamabiraki*) was held here. It doubled as a festival dedicated to Kobo-daishi (774-835), the founder of the Shingon school of esoteric Buddhism, to which Eitaiji belonged. Hiroshige may have named Fukagawa Hachiman here for another reason. The print is dated to the Eighth Month, the fifteenth day of which was the main festival of that shrine. This event was popularly known as *nobori-matsuri* – "the Festival of the Flags".

The "Opening of the Mountain" at the Fukagawa Hachiman Shrine

Fukagawa Hachiman yamabiraki
August 1857
Colour woodblock print, 36 x 24 cm
Gift of Anna Ferris, Brooklyn Museum of Art, New York

147

U p until 1872 Fukagawa could boast a Buddhist temple of unusual shape and function. It was called *Sanjusangendo* – the Thirty-Three-Ken Temple. The *ken* was a measure of length slightly less than six feet, and the name is usually translated in that light. In reality, though, the number referred to the bays between the columns which were two *ken* wide and therefore the gallery was 130 yards long. This is the structure cutting diagonally across the page that Hiroshige places in the foreground.

The Thirty-three Ken Temple in the Fukagawa District

Fukagawa Sanjûsangendo
August 1857
Colour woodblock print, 36 x 24 cm
Brooklyn Museum of Art, New York

Although the print is titled *The Mouth of the Nakagawa River*, in reality it shows the meeting-point of three of Edo's watery arteries: the Nakagawa, Onagigawa and Shinkawa. The Nakagawa (literally "Intermediate River") was an arm of the Tonegawa, which flowed into Edo Bay. The name, according to one version, comes from the fact that it lies between the Tonegawa and the Sumidagawa. The river was noted as an excellent place to fish. In the Edo period, the Nakagawa was used to transport salt, which was mined at Gyotoku by the mouth of the Edogawa.

The Mouth of the Nakagawa River

Nakagawaguchi
February 1857
Colour woodblock print, 36 x 24 cm
Gift of Anna Ferris, Brooklyn Museum of Art, New York

E do was an unusual city. As early as the middle of the eighteenth century it had 1.3 million inhabitants, making it the largest metropolis in the world. Here urban development alternated with extensive rice paddies and orchards, while the rivers were quite heavily fished. The place shown here was noted for its carp – a rare and expensive fish in the Edo period.

"Scattered Pines" on the Bank of the Tonegawa River

Tonegawa barabara matsu
August 1856
Colour woodblock print, 36 x 24 cm
Brooklyn Museum of Art, New York

153

The composition here is unusual, with the legs and arms of a boatman acting as "side-flaps" to the scene. Hairy legs so prominently placed evoke distaste among Western scholars of Hiroshige's work and hence a negative reaction to the print that is not found in Japanese literature about the artist. Indignation would seem out of place here: Hiroshige depicts an entirely typical feature of the locality – a ferryman conveying passengers across the Tamagawa. In the distance we can see a lighthouse marking a sandbar. Behind the trees on the left are the buildings of a shrine dedicated to Benzaiten. Such shrines were often placed on spits, which ran far out into the sea or estuary.

The Benten Shrine by the Haneda-no watashi Ferry

Haneda-no watashi Benten-no yashiro
August 1858
Colour woodblock print, 36 x 24 cm
Gift of Anna Ferris, Brooklyn Museum of Art, New York

155

AUTUMN

The title exactly describes both the content and the atmosphere of the print. *Tanabata-matsuri* – the Festival of the Ox-herd and the Weaver-Girl – is of Chinese origin. It is connected with the ancient legend that the heavenly Weaver-Girl (the star Vega) was separated from her Ox-herd lover (the star Altair), but once a year she was able to meet him by crossing a bridge made by myriads of birds across the Heavenly River (the Milky Way). To the right of Mount Fuji, we can see the buildings of Edo Castle and a little lower the fire-watchtower where Hiroshige was born and lived until the age of thirty-three.

The City Decorated for the Tanabata Festival

Shityu han'ei Tanabata-matsuri
July 1857
Colour woodblock print, 36 x 24 cm
Gift of Anna Ferris, Brooklyn Museum of Art, New York

The procession in the foreground is a *toryo-okuri* – a ritual observed during the building of a new house. After the ridge-piece had been set up, the carpenters performed a ceremony which involved prayers and a banquet. The event ended with a procession in which the carpenters and owners of the new building saw the senior craftsman on his way. This is the moment Hiroshige depicted. This print is among the small number of pure urban landscapes in the series. The theme here is the city, its life and events, not necessarily extraordinary ones.

Fabric Shops in Odemmacho

Odemmachô gofukuten
July 1858
Colour woodblock print, 36 x 24 cm
Gift of Anna Ferris, Brooklyn Museum of Art, New York

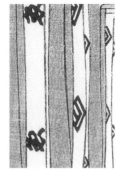

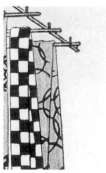

K anda was situated almost in the centre of what is now Chiyoda, the business sector of Tokyo. Kanda became a craftsmen's district, settled by practitioners of a wide range of trades. Kanda was a special place in Edo. It was the cradle of the capital's urban culture, the culture of the *Edokko* who had their own, highly individual view of the world, a system of values and so on that differed in many ways from those officially propagated.

It is no coincidence that many artists, particularly *ukiyo-e* painters, came from here.

The Dyers' Quarter in Kanda

Kanda Kon'yachô
November 1857
Colour woodblock print, 36.9 x 24.8 cm
National Gallery of Australia, Canberra

Kyobashi (literally "the Capital Bridge") stands in the centre of Edo – Tokyo. Yet, like many other sights, it relates to the Tokaido highway. Kyobashi was the first bridge on the traveller's way. After Ieyasu began to organise the new capital, the area around it was settled by representatives of various trades. No less important for the local economy, however, were the businesses that, one way or another, traded in bamboo. Great stocked-up stems of bamboo occupy the whole of the left-hand part of Hiroshige's print.

Two more bridges can be seen in the distance: Nakabashi and Sirauobashi.

The Bamboo Bank by the Kyobashi Bridge

Kyobashi takegashi
December 1857
Colour woodblock print, 36 x 24 cm
Brooklyn Museum of Art, New York

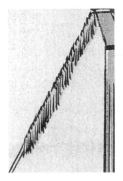

W e look between the masts of two large freight vessels at a canal crossed by a bridge and flanked by buildings of a single type. This is the Hatchobori or "Eight-*cho* Canal" which runs through the central part of old Edo and, at its eastern end, joins the Sumidagawa not far from Edo Bay. The canal was cut in the Kanyei era (1624-1644) and named on account of its length: eight *cho* was about 950 yards. This and other canals were needed because Edo Bay was too shallow to allow large sea-going vessels to come in and moor at piers.

The Minato-jinja Shrine and Inaribashi
Bridge at Teppozu

Teppozu Inaribashi Minato-Jinja
February 1857
Colour woodblock print, 36 x 24 cm
Gift of Anna Ferris, Brooklyn Museum of Art, New York

S outh of the spot depicted in the preceding print lay the Akashicho quarter located on the southern tip of Teppozu. Akashicho was a quiet, unremarkable locality. It was customary to rent houses here and install courtesans redeemed from the "green quarters" in them. Only in the 1870s did Akashicho acquire a distinctive "face" as Europeans began to settle here. The locals made their living by fishing.

The Nishi-Honganji Monastery at Tsukiji, Teppozu

Teppozu Tsukiji monzeki
July 1858
Colour woodblock print, 36 x 24 cm
Gift of Anna Ferris, Brooklyn Museum of Art, New York

The place depicted here is still recognisable today. It is the area in front of the Daimon or Great Gate of the Zojoji monastery, approached by a humpbacked bridge across the Sakuragawa Canal (which joins the Fukagawa nearby). Zojoji was Japan's largest Buddhist centre in the Tokugawa period. In Hiroshige's time the shrine was quite often the venue for theatrical performances. On festivals *sumo* wrestling contests were also held at Shinmei-no miya.

The Shinmei Shrine and the Zojoji Monastery in Shiba

Shiba Shinmei Zojôji
July 1858
Colour woodblock print, 33.5 x 22 cm
Gift of Ines Mottershead, H. C. Carey Collection, Philadelphia

The Kanasugibashi was built where the Tokaido highway crosses the mouth of the Furukawa (known locally as the Kanasugigawa), not far from the entrance to the Zojoji monastery in the Shiba district. Shibaura is the name of a part of that district, the stretch of shore from the mouth of the Furukawa as far as Hama-goten, a palace that at various times belonged to various branches of the Tokugawa family. Almost from the start of the Edo period Shiba was full of Buddhist monasteries.

The Kanasugibashi Bridge and Shibaura

Kanasugibashi Shibaura
July 1857
Colour woodblock print, 36 x 24 cm
Brooklyn Museum of Art, New York

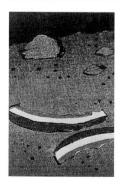

It might seem that the objects placed in the foreground in this print are random and unconnected with each other. In fact, here more than the other works of the series they are apt and symbolic, forming a sort of puzzle, a play on words and images.

In this print too, a fragment of such a conveyance was intended to give a hint of the refined culture of Japanese classical antiquity.

The Ushimachi Quarter in Takanawa

Takanawa Ushimachi
April 1857
Colour woodblock print, 36 x 24 cm
Gift of Anna Ferris, Brooklyn Museum of Art, New York

There are a relatively small number of prints in which the actual landscape view plays a secondary role. This applies, at least to a certain extent, to the present print which shows not so much Edo Bay, seen in the background, as the main room of a teahouse with screen walls (*shoji*) opened. The evening is at an end. It began with the admiration of the full moon, which is the "chief protagonist" of the work, illuminating the view seen through the parted screen walls. The seascape, with boats gliding across the still water of the bay by moonlight, is captivating. Possibly this is the part of Edo Bay close to the Takanawa-no mon Gate.

The Moon above a Headland

Tsuki-no misaki
August 1857
Colour woodblock print, 33.9 x 22.8 cm
The Kelvin Smith Collection, The Cleveland Museum of Art,
Cleveland

In Hiroshige's time the southern district of Shinagawa actually lay outside the city. It was famous for its amusement quarters and as the first staging-post on the Tokaido highway that linked two regions of the main island in the Japanese archipelago – Kanto (with its centre in Edo) and Kansai, whose capital was Kyoto, the residence of the Emperor. Travelling the Tokaido became a fashionable thing to do, a fad which was reflected in literature and the fine arts.

Sandbar in Susaki

Shinagawa Susaki
April 1856
Colour woodblock print, 36 x 24 cm
Brooklyn Museum of Art, New York

H ere we find ourselves at Meguro, a place that was famous for its temple dedicated to Fudo-myoo. A bluff running along the Megurogawa river provides a view far into the distance across rice paddies between which a traveller is leading a horse to the snow-capped summit of Mount Fuji, which was a fine sight from anywhere in Meguro.

"Grandpa's Teahouse" at Meguro

Meguro Jijigachâya
April 1857
Colour woodblock print, 36 x 24 cm
Gift of Anna Ferris, Brooklyn Museum of Art, New York

179

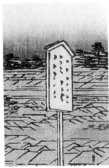

Akasaka was a district adjoining the port. It served as a sort of outpost defending the approaches to the Shogun's residence. In the eighteenth and nineteenth centuries it contained the mansions of *daimyo* – the governors of provinces, among others that of Kii, which gave rise to the name Kinokunizaka, meaning "the slope running along the eastern edge of the mansion of the ruler of Kii". The grounds of this estate have survived to this day, however the mansion itself has been lost. Now the site is occupied by a guesthouse belonging to the Ministry of the Imperial Court, a western-style building.

The Kinokunizaka Slope with the Tameike Pond in Akasaka in the Distance

Kinokunizaka Akasaka Tameike enbo
September 1857
Colour woodblock print, 36 x 24 cm
Gift of Anna Ferris, Brooklyn Museum of Art, New York

Yotsuya was the entrance to the capital from the west. The gate itself is not shown in the print. Even more than the hairy legs, this composition has dismayed connoisseurs of the woodblock print on account of the "vulgar" motif employed. The viewer is asked, as it were, to squat directly under the tail of the horse whose rump occupies three-quarters of the foreground. Here, of course, as with the boatman's legs, we are dealing with Hiroshige's sense of humour. This is a joke, not particularly subtle, but funny in its way and, most importantly, appropriate. The tone wholly accords with the character of the locality depicted.

Naito-Shinjuku in Yotsuya

Yotsuya Naito-Shinjûku
November 1857
Colour woodblock print, 36 x 24 cm
Gift of Anna Ferris, Brooklyn Museum of Art, New York

183

Inokashira-no ike is situated in the middle of the Musashi plain, which, strictly speaking, is not even in the suburbs. The name of the pond means "main source". For many years this aqueduct was the Eastern Capital's only source of drinking water, and it remained an important source right up to the Meiji period.

We have a view across the pond to the distant Nikko chain including Nantaisan on the left, a celebrated peak that was poetically termed the Fuji of Nikko.

The Benten Shrine on Inokashira-no ike Pond

Inokashira-no ike Benten-no yashiro
April 1856
Colour woodblock print, 34 x 22.5 cm
Gift of Ines Mottershead
H.C. Carey Collection, Philadelphia

井の頭の池弁天の社

Takinogawa means "the river of waterfalls" and one might well think that it is the name of the river shown in the print. In actual fact we are looking here at a section of the Shakujiigawa that runs through the Oji district. Throughout the Edo period this was a rural area, some five miles distant from the city centre, that grew vegetables for sale in the capital's markets.

Takinogawa in Oji

Oji Takinogawa
April 1856
Colour woodblock print, 36 x 24 cm
Gift of Anna Ferris, Brooklyn Museum of Art, New York

187

Hiroshige takes us back to the monastery at Ueno and right up to the tree that the *Edokko* called Tsuki-no matsu – "the moon pine". In Hiroshige's print, the view through the Moon Pine is of Shinobazu-no ike, the "impatient pond". There are two areas of buildings beyond the tree. The nearer one is on the island of Nakajima, which was artificially created almost in the middle of the pond. The opposite shore of the pond (Hongodai) was occupied in Hiroshige's time by the mansions of *daimyo*.

The "Moon Pine" in the Precincts of the Monastery at Ueno

Ueno sannai Tsuki-no matsu
August 1857
Colour woodblock print, 33.9 x 22.5 cm
Achenbach Foundation for Graphic Arts, Fine Arts Museums
of San Francisco, San Francisco

189

In this series Hiroshige devotes much attention to the "green quarters" of Yoshiwara and to the routes by which they are reached. This was quite natural. Yoshiwara was a focal point of the distinctive urban culture, a centre with a tremendous attraction for all the inhabitants of the Eastern Capital and for visitors. The only attraction that could rival it was the *Kabuki* theatre, a new form of performance art that appeared and developed in the Edo period. As with all other aspects of life, the Tokugawa government strictly regulated everything connected with the theatre.

The Saruwakamachi Quarter by Night

Saruwakamachi yoru-no kei
September 1856
Colour woodblock print, 36 x 24 cm
Gift of Anna Ferris, Brooklyn Museum of Art, New York

191

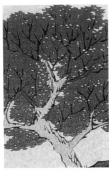

The scarlet leaves of the maple are a sign of autumn in many parts of the world, but in Japan especially, much attention was devoted to the changing colours of foliage. It became a profound aesthetic experience, a theme of poetry and painting. Naturally maples featured in the "autumnal" section of Hiroshige's series, but only in this print has the colour effect that the artist intended survived down to the present day. Different red pigments were used here that did not decompose and darken to the point of complete blackness as in two other autumnal prints in the series.

In the Precincts of the Akiba Shrine at Ukeji

Ukeji Akiba-no keidai
August 1857
Colour woodblock print, 36 x 24 cm
Brooklyn Museum of Art, New York

Hardly anything of what is "promised" in the title actually appears in the print: The main sight of this area is the Mokuboji monastery, in whose grounds Uehan stood, but its buildings are not shown. The monastery was founded in the Jogan era (976-978). Its name is inseparably associated with the sad story of Umewakamaru, the young son of a courtier, who was kidnapped by a slave trader and taken far away. The boy was not up to such a journey and died on the road of hunger and privations. The local villagers buried him and planted a willow on his grave. A wandering monk built a prayer-house alongside that later developed into the monastery.

The Mokuboji Monastery, the Uchigawa River and the Gozensaihata Fields

Mokuboji Uchigawa Gozensaihata
December 1857
Colour woodblock print, 37 x 24.5 cm
Joy Swann Collection

195

There were many ferries in Edo; indeed they were perhaps the most important means of transport within the city, and Hiroshige depicted them repeatedly. Only in this print, however, does the artist show us a ferry landing, the place where crossings start and finish. This is the landing of the Niijuku ferry that crossed the Nakagawa, an arm of the Tonegawa that flowed into Edo Bay.

The Niijuku-no watashi Ferry

Niijûku-no watashi
February 1857
Colour woodblock print, 36 x 24 cm
Brooklyn Museum of Art, New York

The diverse, skilfully constructed landscape is shown from between the forked branches of a large maple, whose scarlet leaves hang down right in front of the viewer's eyes. This remarkable tree was for a long time the main sight of the whole area. This immense maple – two men could not embrace its trunk – grew in the precincts of Guhoji, a monastery with an ancient history. The grounds of the monastery had a reputation as a fine place to admire the autumnal foliage, mainly due to this one tree.

Scarlet Maple Trees at Mama by the Tekona-no yashiro Shrine and the Tsugihashi Bridge

Mama-no momiji Tekona-no yachting Tsugihashi
January 1857
Colour woodblock print, 35.1 x 24.2 cm
Arthur M. Sackler Museum, Gift of the Friends of Arthur B. Duel
Harvard University Art Museums, Cambridge, MA

Konodai is still one of the best places from which to view Mount Fuji. This hill, dropping precipitously to the Tonegawa river, is strongly associated with Japan's warlike past.

The hill was very valuable from a military point of view, since whoever held it could control an extensive area. Consequently the top of the hill was fortified.

In the Edo period the hill itself changed shape due to a landslide, leaving a cliff-like slope above the Tonegawa. This was the best spot for viewing Mount Fuji, just as three figures in the print are doing.

View of Konodai Hill and the Tonegawa River

Konodai Tonegawa fukei
May 1856
Colour woodblock print, 36 x 24 cm
Brooklyn Museum of Art, New York

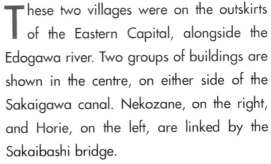

These two villages were on the outskirts of the Eastern Capital, alongside the Edogawa river. Two groups of buildings are shown in the centre, on either side of the Sakaigawa canal. Nekozane, on the right, and Horie, on the left, are linked by the Sakaibashi bridge.

As well as fishing and gathering shellfish, the local inhabitants also occasionally hunted birds. In the foreground we can see one of the methods that they used.

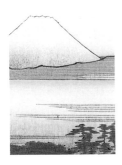

Horie and Nekozane

Horie Nekozane
February 1856
Colour woodblock print, 36.4 x 24.5 cm
Robert O. Muller Collection, New York

Many place names in old Edo were connected with trees, pine-trees in particular, probably because they were perceived as symbols of longevity. Among such place names is Gohonmatsu, which literally means "five pines". At one time there were indeed five trees here, but by the early nineteenth century four had been lost. The remaining tree, which grew in the grounds of the Kuki mansion, survived until the end of the century. The unusual shape of the old pine attracted people's attention and became a local sight.

The "Gohonmatsu Pine" on the Onagigawa Canal

Onagigawa Gohonmatsu
July 1856
Colour woodblock print, 34.1 x 22.2 cm
Carlotta Mabury Collection, Fine Arts Museums of San
Francisco, San Francisco

The spectacle we witness here can be taken as a precise, symbolic expression of the essence of Edo's urban culture – the last and most individual manifestation of traditional Japanese culture. This is a night view with the dark sky occupying almost two-thirds of the picture, yet the scene is brightly lit by a glittering display of aerial fireworks. The Ryogokubashi was a special place in the capital. The bridge itself was built in 1659-1661 to the design of the government officials Shibayama Genyemon and Tsubouchi Tozaemon. All sorts of amusements, celebrations and festivities took place around the bridge – on land and on the water.

Fireworks by the Ryogokubashi Bridge

Ryogoku hanabi
August 1858
Colour woodblock print, 33.7 x 22 cm
Bequest of James Parmelee, Cleveland Museum of Art, Cleveland

207

WINTER

Kinryuzan (literally "the mountain of the golden dragon") was one of the three oldest and most important centres of Buddhism in the Eastern Capital. It was founded in the 36th year of Empress Suiko's reign (627) when the religion was still taking its first steps in Japan. The best period for Sensoji, as the monastery was more often called, began in 1589 when Tokugawa Ieyasu took notice of it. Sensoji retained firm ties with the ruling family. Its popularity was also greatly bolstered by the fact that it stood alongside the Eastern Capital's most celebrated pleasure quarters.

The Kinryuzan Monastery in Asakusa

Asakusa Kinryuzan
July 1856
Colour woodblock print, 35.7 x 24.1 cm
The Howard Mansfield Collection,
The Metropolitan Museum of Art, New York

In the series, the artist thoroughly traces the route leading to the famous "green quarters" of Yoshiwara. The journey was a long one, and the last stretch of it ran alongside the Sanyabori canal. Here, by the Imadobashi Bridge, the pleasure-seeker disembarked from the small boat that had usually been hired by the Yanagibashi and continued on foot or in a palanquin. The embankment, or more precisely dyke, along the canal appeared in the first half of the seventeenth century, following the flood that seriously affected the Asakusa district in 1619.

The Nihonzutsumi Embankment at Yoshiwara

Yoshiwara Nihonzutsumi
April 1857
Colour woodblock print, 33.8 x 22.2 cm
Gift of Anna Ferris
Brooklyn Museum of Art, New York

In this print we find ourselves upstairs in one of the pleasure houses of Yoshiwara. The room is in a state of slight disorder. A towel decorated with a feather motif is carelessly draped on the windowsill, creating the impression that it has just been used. Next to the towel is a bowl for rinsing the mouth. There seems to be no-one in the room, but the presence of its mistress is clearly sensed. In all probabilities, she is behind the screen.

The Torinomachi Pilgrimage in the Asakusa Rice Paddies

Asakusa tambo Torinomachi mode
November 1857
Colour woodblock print, 36 x 24 cm
Gift of Anna Ferris, Brooklyn Museum of Art, New York

The three villages mentioned were next to Yoshiwara on the one side, and on the other adjoined the Oshukaido, the highway that connected the capital to the northern provinces.

Although all three villages were incorporated into the capital in 1745, the area remained rural throughout the Edo period. The Shogun came here to hunt with falcons. The objects of the hunt were the cranes shown in the foreground of the print. From ancient times in China, and then in Japan, the crane was regarded as a symbol of longevity, the companion of the Taoist immortals (*hsian*) and their embodiment.

The Villages of Minowa, Kanasugi and Mikawashima

Minowa Kanasugi Mikawashima
May 1857
Colour woodblock print, 33.8 x 21.8 cm
Carlotta Mabury Collection, Fine Arts Museums of San Francisco, San Francisco

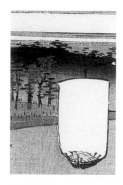

The Sumidagawa was the main river of the Eastern Capital; the Senju-Ohashi was the first, and largest, bridge over the river. Concerned with domestic stability, the Tokugawa government did not, in principle, encourage the construction of bridges across major rivers, but the traffic between Edo and the northern provinces of Honshu island was exceptionally intensive and a bridge across the Sumidagawa, connecting the centre of the city with the Oshukaido highway leading northwards, was a necessity. It was built in 1594 using the evergreen wood *inumaki* which is resistant to rot.

The Ohashi Bridge in Senju

Senjû-no Ohashi
February 1856
Colour woodblock print, 36 x 24 cm
Gift of Anna Ferris
Brooklyn Museum of Art, New York

217

This locality, on the east bank of the Sumidagawa, was far from lively, perhaps even somewhat cheerless. The village lay in the Honjo district, about two-and-a-half miles from the city centre. At one time it was the location of a mansion belonging to the Mito clan, a side branch of the Tokugawa house. Koume and the surrounding area also acquired a certain fame from the Hikifunegawa canal, on the bank of which Hiroshige places us.

The Koume Embankment

Koumezutsumi
February 1857
Colour woodblock print, 36 x 24 cm
Gift of Anna Ferris, Brooklyn Museum of Art, New York

O mmayagashi was on the western bank of the Sumidagawa to the north of the government rice-stores. The name, and that of the Ommaya-no watashi, can be translated as "stables embankment" and "stables ferry", which exactly describes their location, since up until the 1790s the adjoining quarter was occupied by the Shogun's stables. The ferry was in frequent use. It was allocated eight boats, one of which is approaching the bank in the foreground. The passengers are two prostitutes (*yotaka*, literally "night-hawks") and their bodyguard, a *gyu* ("bull-calf").

The Ommayagashi Embankment

Ommayagashi
December 1857
Colour woodblock print, 33.3 x 21.8 cm
Gift of Patricia Brown McNamara, Jane Brown Dunaway,
and Helen Brown Jarman
Fine Arts Museums of San Francisco, San Francisco

The composition is based on the sketches Hiroshige made from life: the image is enclosed by the logs crossing the picture diagonally and by the lines of the hill descending to the canal. The result is a sort of diamond-shaped frame through which we see the snow-covered banks and trees, the rafts on the water and the dark wintry sky with a sprinkling of falling snow. The "keystone" of this frame takes the form of an open bamboo umbrella bearing the character for "fish", *uo*, which is the first part of Uoei, the publisher's abbreviated name. His stamp is placed alongside, at the bottom of the left-hand margin.

The Fukagawa Timberyards

Fukagawa kiba
August 1856
Colour woodblock print, 36 x 24 cm
Gift of Anna Ferris, Brooklyn Museum of Art, New York

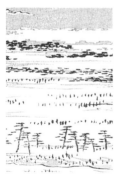

Jumantsubo – "one hundred thousand tsubo" (a *tsubo* was roughly four square yards) – was an area of marshland reclaimed in the 1720s, and Mount Tsukuba on the horizon. In the mid-nineteenth century Jumantsubo contained the suburban residence of one of the *daimyo*. The landscape is deserted and the hand of man only hinted at. The place "belongs" to the gigantic eagle hovering in the winter skies above this vast emptiness. The bird is symbolic; it is probably an allusion to the deity of the Washi-daimyojin shrine, which was also linked to the New Year.

Susaki and Jumantsubo in Fukagawa

Fukagawa Susaki Jûmantsubo
May 1857
Colour woodblock print, 35.8 x 23.5 cm
Gift of Harvey Eagleson, Los Angeles County Museum of Art,
Los Angeles

H ere we see the part where the small Shimbashigawa enters the bay. On the southern, man-made sandbar that covered an area of sixty acres, stood the Hamagoten palace. Its grounds with some buildings are shown on the right, the shoreline reinforced with stone walls. Originally the palace belonged to a lesser branch of the Tokugawa family, before passing to the ruling line. It remained a residence of the Shogun up until the Meiji revolution of 1868. In 1870 it was converted for the reception of noble foreigners.

View of Shibaura Inlet

Shibaura-no fukei
February 1857
Colour woodblock print, 36 x 24 cm
Brooklyn Museum of Art, New York

S amezu was the part of the shoreline of Edo Bay, slightly less than a mile long, between the fringes of the Shinagawa district and the mouth of the Tachikawa river. The main peculiarity of Samezu was its plantations of *nori*, an edible seaweed. It was grown in a special fashion: in the autumn, tree branches were stuck into the shallow bottom in long rows. They became entangled with seaweed as it grew and the harvest could be gathered at low tide in winter and spring. The boats in the foreground are steering between the stands of branches.

The Samezu Coast and Minami-Shinagawa

Minami-Shinagawa Samezu kaigan
February 1857
Colour woodblock print, 36 x 24 cm
Gift of Anna Ferris, Brooklyn Museum of Art, New York

The pond depicted here was at one time quite extensive, but by the first half of the nineteenth century it had shrunk to three *cho* (about 360 yards) from west to east and fifty-five yards from north to south. In the depths of a grove on the right bank of the pond we can see the Shinto shrine Senzoku Hachimangu. This locality is associated with Nichiren (1222-1282), the founder of one of the most popular schools of Buddhism. The pine tree fenced-off on the right bank of the pond is called Kesakakematsu – "the hanging robe pine".

The "Kesakakematsu Pine" by the Senzoku-no ike Pond

———

Senzoku-no ike Kesakakematsu
February 1856
Colour woodblock print, 36 x 24 cm
Gift of Anna Ferris, Brooklyn Museum of Art, New York

名所江戸百景
千束の池袈裟懸松

The hill was in Meguro, close to the main sight of the district — the Fudo temple, which for reasons that remain unclear Hiroshige did not depict in any of the prints of the series. Behind the hill was a small Buddhist temple called Myooin, approached by the path leading from the bridge on the left. The bridge itself is, however, the semantic and compositional centre of the print. Despite the fact that stone structures rarely lasted long in Edo with its frequent earthquakes, the bridge in Meguro survived from the 1740s at least into the late 1850s, of which this print is itself proof.

The Taikobashi Bridge and Yuhinooka Hill in Meguro

Meguro Taikobashi Yuhinooka
April 1857
Colour woodblock print, 36 x 24 cm
Gift of Anna Ferris, Brooklyn Museum of Art, New York

Atagoshita was a place in the Minato district below Mount Atago. The hill is to the right and in the distance we can see the red gate marking the start of the ascent to the Atago-jinja shrine. It was one of the aristocratic areas of the city, containing the mansions of influential *daimyo*. Hiroshige places us here on Yabukoji, but we are looking at another street that runs alongside the Sakuragawa canal near the Zojoji monastery towards the Toranomon Gate. The name Yabukoji came from thickets of bamboo, and in the right foreground we see the end of a hedge of the great grass.

Yabukoji Lane at Atagoshita

Atagoshita Yabukoji
December 1857
Colour woodblock print, 36 x 24 cm
Gift of Anna Ferris, Brooklyn Museum of Art, New York

235

The Toranomon Gate stood in the very centre of Edo, close to Kasumigaseki and the Outer Moat of the castle. The name means "tiger gate" and, as is often the case, there are various explanations for it. Toranomon was built in 1614 and stood until 1873. The tree at the top is one of the *enoki*, iron-trees, that grew in large numbers here and gave their name to another slope that runs leftwards from this tree. This is considered one of the most attractive winter scenes in Hiroshige's series.

The Aoizaka Slope beyond the Toranomon Gate

Toranomon-soto Aoizaka
November 1857
Colour woodblock print, 36 x 24 cm
Gift of Anna Ferris, Brooklyn Museum of Art, New York

This bridge stood in the very centre of Edo, spanning the Kyobashi river at the point where it flowed into the Sotobori, the Outer Moat of the castle. The bridge was in the very heart of Edo's commercial and manufacturing life, yet the immediate area had a rather dubious reputation reflected in the name of the bridge. Literally it means "Nuns' Bridge", but the *bikuni* referred to were low-class prostitutes, one small step up from the *yotaka*. They got this colloquial name because they dressed like Buddhist nuns. Hiroshige depicts an ordinary, everyday scene of city life here. In the distance we see a fire-watchtower, an invariable feature of the Eastern Capital, particularly near the centre.

The Bikunibashi Bridge in a Snow Shower

Bikunibashi seishû
October 1857
Colour woodblock print, 36 x 24 cm
Gift of Anna Ferris, Brooklyn Museum of Art, New York

E do appeared as a military city and samurai made up at least half of its population. Times changed and under the Tokugawa dynasty Japan entered a prolonged period of peace. The moral and professional degeneration of the martial class became a danger and the government devoted much attention to instilling in the samurai the ethical standards of the *bushido*, the "way of the warrior" and maintaining their military preparedness. With this aim, several riding-grounds were created in Edo. The first was Takata-no baba, constructed in 1636 in a north-western suburb of the Eastern Capital.

The Takata Riding Ground

Takata-no baba
February 1857
Colour woodblock print, 36 x 24 cm
Brooklyn Museum of Art, New York

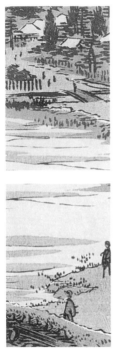

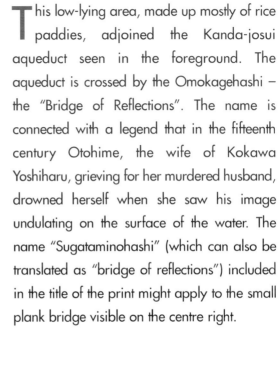

This low-lying area, made up mostly of rice paddies, adjoined the Kanda-josui aqueduct seen in the foreground. The aqueduct is crossed by the Omokagehashi – the "Bridge of Reflections". The name is connected with a legend that in the fifteenth century Otohime, the wife of Kokawa Yoshiharu, grieving for her murdered husband, drowned herself when she saw his image undulating on the surface of the water. The name "Sugataminohashi" (which can also be translated as "bridge of reflections") included in the title of the print might apply to the small plank bridge visible on the centre right.

The Sugataminohashi Bridge, Omokagenohashi Bridge and the Jariba Quarter

Omokagenohashi Jâriba
January 1857
Colour woodblock print, 36 x 24 cm
Gift of Anna Ferris, Brooklyn Museum of Art, New York

H ere we are back in the very centre of old Edo, looking at the Shinobazu-no ike Pond, in the middle of which was the famous shrine of Benzaiten, the water deity and goddess of happiness. On the opposite bank we can see the red buildings of Kanyeiji.

Hiroshige places us alongside the red *torii* gate marking the entrance to a shrine called Yushima Tenjin or Yushima Temmangu.

View from the Tenjin Shrine Hill at Yushima

Yushima Tenjin sakaue tenbo
April 1856
Colour woodblock print, 34.2 x 22.7 cm
Gift of Patricia Brown McNamara, Jane Brown Dunaway,
and Helen Brown Jarman
Fine Arts Museums of San Francisco, San Francisco

245 の の の の の の の の の の

This print depicts neither a monastery, nor a shrine or a hill, waterfall or bridge. It does not depict any festival, although the subject is related to the chief festival of all four seasons – the New Year, more precisely its approach. Edo is presented in a "strange" aspect: the artist plunges into the world of ghosts and transformed creatures, the realm beyond. The spot was called Shozoku-bata (Shozoku Fields). Both the settlement and the field are quite recognisable, but the subject of the print is not them, rather the belief that gave them their name. It is the *enoki*, iron-tree, standing in the centre and the host of vixens accompanied by mysterious tongues of flame (*kitsunebi*).

"Fox Fires" by the Iron Tree at Oji

Oji Shôzoku enoki omisoka no kitsunebi
September 1857
Colour woodblock print, 33.5 x 23.4 cm
The Newark Museum, Newark

List of Illustrations

G

H

I

K